The Laws
of
REVIVAL

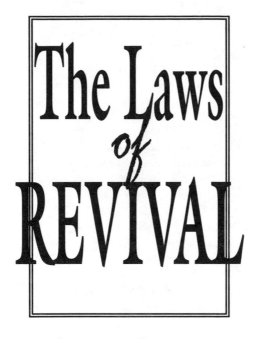

The Laws of REVIVAL

James Burns

Edited by
Tom Phillips

World Wide Publications

The Laws of Revival
by James Burns, edited by Tom Phillips
© 1992, 1993 Billy Graham Evangelistic Association
Used by permission.

Published by World Wide Publications 1993
in cooperation with the Institute of Evangelism,
Billy Graham Center, Wheaton, IL.

ISBN: 0-89066-240-1
Printed in the United States of America

*Our thanks to
Alisa Johnson, Kathy Maas, and
Ralph Williams for their assistance
in the preparation of this booklet.*

Contents

Foreword

Periodically in the history of the Christian Church a work is produced which transcends time. *Revivals, Their Laws and Leaders* by James Burns was written in 1909 and last published in 1960.

Though it is out of print, portions of the book, especially the sections on "The Laws of Revival," are so pertinent today that they literally cry out for editing and republishing.

"If my people, who are called by my name, will humble themselves and pray and seek my face and turn from their wicked ways, then will I hear from heaven and will forgive their sin and will heal their land" (2 Chronicles 7:14, NIV).

As the above Scripture encourages us regarding awakening in our time, so will this booklet. We pray that it will be a tremendous blessing to you in your ministry as you read it.

May an expectation for true spiritual revival come as we sense in reading this wonderful spiritual treatise that the world in which we live today is ripe for a new, profound movement of God's Spirit, perhaps one that has already begun.

May you be encouraged.
Sincerely,

Tom Phillips
Director of Counseling and Follow-Up
Billy Graham Evangelistic Association

Introduction

In Christian history, no phenomenon is more clear than the recurrence of revivals.

At times, a passion for repentance sweeps across specific geographical areas. Many people who had been unaware of the supernatural become keenly aware of it. They are stopped during their jobs as their minds are gripped by a terror of wrongdoing and a fear of coming judgment. Throwing all else aside, they desperately search for a way of salvation.

Having started, these movements spread like wildfire and are seemingly carried in the air. Breaking out in unexpected places, they produce a strange phenomenon and awaken forces that have lain dormant. Mostly, these movements are contained in a local geographic area, but they can spread throughout nations, with incredible results.

Since revivals are a major characteristic of Christianity, a study of church growth and survival would be worthless if it ignored the impact of revivals.

In light of this, we cannot regard revivals as isolated incidents. To interpret the mind and will of God in relation to humanity, we need to look at the permanent elements of human nature and the underlying laws which shape human history. Such movements witness to us the supremacy of spiritual forces. They reveal the spiritual instincts in humankind that are often clouded by less worthwhile pursuits. They encourage faith by showing God's hand in history and in His guidance of the Church. These movements prove that God is working through His laws, for the salvation of His people and for the world's good.

In a revival, a few, then dozens, then thousands say with David, "Though I walk in the midst of trouble, You will revive me" (Psalm 138:7, NKJV).

1

Revivals, the Law of Progress

We need to acknowledge the part revivals play in God's plan as we take a broader look and see them appear in places outside of the Church. Progress, we see, occurs through revival. Any progress is like the incoming tide. Each wave is a revival, going forward, receding, and being followed by another. To the onlooker it seems as if nothing is gained, but the force behind the ebb and flow is the power of the tide. So it is with the nations. One will rise and carry human progress to a zenith. Having done so, it falls back, and another replaces it. Thus, the progress of humanity is continued through successive revivals.

The same is true in all realms of human expression. When new discoveries are made, the scientific outlook captivates people's minds and other areas are put on the back burner. But nothing can totally dominate the mind. The initial force eventually fades. After making its contribution to human knowledge and making life better by its discoveries, the movement gives way and is replaced by another in a different area.

Each outburst has its own characteristics and direction, but its nature is revival. There is an excitement in an area, a gathering of energy to leap forward, and when its strength is spent, it recedes. This is even seen in commerce. Trade depressions are succeeded by trade revivals, and in the world market there is a constant ebb and flow.

In all this, we can see God's wisdom. Revivals are necessary to push humankind to higher planes. If progress were uniform, with all aspects of life improving at once, advancement would be so slow that life would stagnate. There would be no high hopes, no eager rush forward. Progress would be imperceptible— and men and women, robbed of aspirations, would give up the fight. By the breath of fresh life, God keeps the world active and keeps the heart fresh with hope. In God's purposes, no part of human nature is left unrevived. Each revival is needed for helping human nature. Their order is God's secret, the equilibrium is in His hands. Behind the ebb and flow is the unrelenting tide of His redemptive purposes. He it is who said, "Let all the world look to me for salvation!" (Isaiah 45:22, TLB).

2

Revivals, the Law of Spiritual Growth

Revivals are the method by which progress occurs in all other realms of human expression. In light of this, we can approach their recurrence in religion free from bias, and even scorn, which has been popularly considered the right attitude. It is in this area that the word *revival* gains a new intensity, for religion deals with the awesome and unmeasurable. It goes deep into men's and women's spiritual consciousness. As interesting as other revivals may be, they are shadows when compared with the importance of revivals in the individual and the Church. Though they occur in this mysterious realm, they are not necessarily erratic or arbitrary. The supreme discovery is that nothing is erratic in God's universe. Characteristics common to all revivals may be found.

When we examine revivals in the spiritual life, we are confronted with a mass of interesting material. Revivals are used of God to stimulate individual and corporate spiritual life and to advance spiritual education and progress. They are characterized with the same frequency and fluctuations as revivals in other areas.

First, we discover fluctuations in the common experience of men and women before decisions about Christianity are made. Let's remember back before your conversion. There were times when you were conscious of definite, spiritual influences moving you powerfully to Him. Then there were long periods in which you seemed to have no consciousness of any spiritual pressure. After months—or even years—of spiritual lethargy, the influence would return.

This ebb and flow of spiritual experience is still characteristic in life after conversion. No life is maintained at the same level. The Psalms reveal the varying nature of the divine life in the believer's heart. Caught by the inflowing wave, the writer's heart rejoices in God. Then in the trough of the wave, the Psalmist cries out for help, with his heart in despair. From this, God rescues him. He is then carried forward on a new tide of joy.

This same experience characterizes all Christian church life. The spiritual life within any congregation is never constant. Each church has times of being a spiritual desert, followed by times of awakening and revival. Even in the first century Church the believers longed for greater manifestations of God's word and power (Acts 4:23–31).

Progress never occurs in an unbroken sequence. The pressure of the Holy Spirit upon the life of an individual and the Church is never uniform. The reason is not difficult to discover. A constant pressure becomes a mere condition of our life. We adjust to it, without its attracting our attention, but a pressure that is occasional and variable captivates our attention. The Holy Spirit demonstrates His sovereignty in nurturing change in us and captivates our interest by varying His influence at different times, for it is by this method that the conscience is reached and the heart is won.

In the influx of the tide, there are not only tiny ripples, but also tumultuous waves and mighty breakers. In the inflowing tide of human spiritual progress there is the same variety of waves. There are revivals which affect the individual. There are larger movements which affect separate congregations, and even larger ones that affect whole geographical areas and spread beyond.

The history of revivals reveals large movements, infrequent in their appearance, but monumental in their character. They change life's conditions and deeply alter the history of the world. In looking at some of these movements, we discover certain laws which govern their activity. How they work becomes more apparent, the effect more convincing and overpowering. For what is common to all great movements is present in small ones.

3

Revivals,
the Law of Periodicity

We may assume that revivals are one of the primary methods God uses to fulfill His purposes in the world. These revivals move according to a divine law. There is an orderly sequence in their movements. But can we discover this sequence? Do revivals recur at definite intervals? Can we forecast their appearance, as astronomers forecast the appearance of a comet? Obviously, this is impossible. The movements cannot be treated as an exact science. Human life does not move with precision. The wills of men and women enter, with all their inconstancy. The unexpected occurs, which changes the course of events. While these cannot stop God's plan, they may retard it.

It is impossible for us to map out with precision the recurrence of revivals. This does not mean that all that pertains to them is hidden away in the unsearchable purposes of God. It is clear that their appearance at specific times is not haphazard. One's spiritual nature is not allowed to stagnate for long periods. Neither do revivals rush upon men and women at random, without preparation or purpose. A certain law of periodicity is discernible. Even though we cannot prophesy with unerring accuracy their arrival, we can at least know that behind them is divine law and order.

4

Revivals,
the Law of Ebbing Tide

We find preceding each revival a spiritual desert. During those times, all whose hearts are alienated and are skeptical of the Church's authority break away. In those dark days unbelief reigns while the enfeebled Church, without the strength to fight back, sits in humiliating impotence.

The Church is not blameless. The loss of hope is due to the loss of spiritual power. The loss of spiritual power is the result of leaving the heart of the Church unprotected against the world. Individually, we see this when our hearts are left in such a state. As the inner fire ceases to glow, the warmth departs. We still act like Christians. In fact, we may even look more spiritual in our effort to cover up our spiritual decay. Since the Spirit is not there, we are only offering lip service to God. The length of relapse will depend upon the character of each person. In some, because of their intense spirituality, the ebb and flow will be faint. In others, the waves will be strong and violent.

In those large movements thrown upon

pages of human history, we see these facts magnified. The defection of the individual spreads until it reaches the Church. In the lowered spiritual state, corruption creeps in until finally the whole body is permeated with worldliness. Each generation has its own level of corruption. Thus, it would be wrong to say that revival will not occur because the corruption is not the same as previously. There is ebb and flow, but it is that of a constantly advancing tide. Yet the extent of the falling away may be great, for the fall has to be measured from the fresh advance which has been reached. Each age receives the renewed perception of God's standard of righteousness. Each age also develops its own standard of judgment. But it is according to God's standard that the Church may be condemned for defection.

5

Revivals, the Law of the Fullness of Time

The next fact which the study of revival discloses is that this time of spiritual deadness has its definite limits. The wave of spiritual progress recedes, but even in receding it is gathering in power and volume to return, and to rush further in. God has set a limit to the defection of His Church. When the night is at its darkest, the dawn is on the way.

This next period is characterized by a dissatisfaction in many hearts. A period of gloom sets in; a weariness and exhaustion invades the heart. The pleasures of the world no longer satisfy. Thus, men and women turn to God. They realize that, in exchanging heavenly for earthly joys, they have encountered immense loss. Slowly this aching grows, the hearts of people begin to cry out to God. From a faint desire, this multiplies until it becomes a vast human need, until, in its urgency, it seems to beat at the very gates of heaven.

Within the Church, not all have fallen away. Some have mourned its loss of spiritual power and have never stopped earnestly praying for revival. Their prayer seems to go unanswered. It appears as if God has forgotten to be gracious. Gradually, the number of people praying increases. Prayer becomes more urgent and more confident. The condition of the Church becomes apparent. The need increasingly weighs upon the hearts of the devout. The longing for better things becomes an intense pain. People form into prayer groups. They do not cease imploring God to visit the souls of men and women. In many different places, unconnected with each other, this spirit of intercession awakens. With it comes an expectation that will not be denied, a premonition that there are better days ahead.

Times of awakening in the individual mostly occur at times of transition, especially from one stage of development to another. Spiritual awakenings coincide with profound change in the social or political life of the people. The value of this is apparent, since new energies are conserved, and directed into channels which will lead to true progress.

The twelfth century saw Europe passing out of the Middle Ages. The feudal system was breaking up, and people were gathering in cities. A new sense of corporate life was emerging. Individuals were grouping themselves in wider combinations. Papal absolutism, which had held individuals' minds in subjection, was beginning to lose its grip. It was losing its power because of the growing independence of secular authorities and the irritation growing from newly awakened intelligence. At this time, universities began to spring up. There was a widening of sympathies, due to the Crusades and the ferment of new ideas, thus marking the close of one stage of human development and the beginning of another.

When we come to the next great movement, we stand again at a crisis in human affairs. Europe, which had in the previous period passed from childhood into youth, was in the sixteenth century passing from youth to maturity. Loyalty to the city was giving way to loyalty to the state. Europe was rearranging itself under modern geographical and national divisions. It was the time of the awakening of learning and art. Here again we see one stage of growth completed and a fresh stage beginning.

After the sixteenth century, revivals shifted to the national level, since each nation differed in its stage of development. Also at this time, the Reformation had destroyed the unity and the control of Rome. Still, in these more limited movements, revival synchronizes with crises in development.

Thus, we see how at times all things seem to unite and cry out for a revival. The waters are far withdrawn and heaped up, foaming behind the barricade. The times are ripe. The soul of humankind cries out for God. A spirit of intense expectation is present. Once more the long bitter night has ended; the dawn is at hand.

6

Revivals, the Law of the Advent of the Prophet

The next event common to the history of all great revivals is the appearance of a leader. The person sums up in himself or herself the longings of the time and interprets to the generation their inmost needs. When this person speaks, the hearers recognize his or her authority.

In this sense, the leader is recognized not as the creator but as the interpreter of the movement. The burden of the times, which others only faintly feel, becomes an intolerable load. The leader feels God's hand upon him or her and proceeds—possessed by the Holy Spirit— to be God's agent in leading men and women into new life.

Though the agent and the interpreter, the leader is not a machine. The leader brings into the movement his or her own individuality, and within certain limits defines its characteristics. When we survey the leaders in the world's revivals, we see how wide the selection is, how varied the characters of God's chosen servants. For example, Isaiah and Paul were separated by more than centuries. The same wide difference may be seen in the movements themselves because the characteristics of the movements are marked by their leaders. These characteristics were essential for the success of the movement, because each age has different needs the leader can meet.

Here the differences end. All of these great leaders share an unshakable faith in God, an overwhelming sense of a call to service, a mysterious equipment of spiritual power, and a determination to do the work of God at the expense of life itself.

7

Revivals,
the Law of Awakening

When these elements of preparation, timing, and leadership fall into place, the awakening occurs. The people that walked in darkness see a great light. They fling off the garments of despair and celebrate life.

In each movement there is something incalculable. New forces, long preparing under the surface, burst into being. The revival's tide rolls in from an unseen continent and moves with a gathering, unresisting momentum. Yet while each is individual, there is uniformity.

Each revival is characterized by the extraordinary swiftness with which it spreads. Once the first words of the new message are spoken, mysterious forces arise, like the wind, and carry them from place to place. The revival spreads like an epidemic. It bursts out in places that have not been in contact with other infected places, and individuals are moved in multitudes.

Luther's nailing of the 98 Theses on the church door at Wittenberg seemed to be of little importance, but it was a spark to a dry forest, and the fire that it began has yet to be put out. When Wesley stood up in the open air to address a crowd of illiterate miners, no one knew that it would be the beginning of one of the largest Protestant churches in the world. The rapidity with which revivals spread is an indication of the silent preparation which goes on beneath the surface long before the revival itself takes place. It shows how God's Spirit is always active.

Everyone who studies the phenomena of revivals is struck by the similarity of the effects produced upon those who are touched by them. Two of these stand out with startling vividness and are common to all.

First of all is the deep conviction of sin. In the intense spiritual light, the sin and guilt of the awakened soul stand out in terrifying blackness. Not only are their sins laid bare, but the convicted see themselves as in a mirror. Every sin, seemingly minor, confronts them. Their sin drags them to judgment. Terror seizes them as the conviction of sin burns like fire. Yet this terror of the Lord is not the terror of punishment. It is inspired by a sense of having rebelled against God.

Under this agony of conviction, men and women openly confess their sins. Their one intense longing is to cast their sins forever from them, to be brought into reconciliation and peace with God. Even those who are only attracted by curiosity feel the irresistible power dragging them to confession. Some, though totally ignorant of spiritual things, are brought to conversion.

The dulled conscience has permitted many things to creep within the Church's doors. They might not be wrong in themselves, but tend to dull the edge of its spiritual life. When the inner fires cease to glow with love for Christ, there is nothing left to defend the Church from the world. In many cases, divisions arise or worship is reduced to cold formalities. Worldly practices are permitted in order to maintain interest. Although they are condemned by many, there is not the power to eject them. The Church becomes worldly, selfish, and almost Christless.

With a revival, all this is changed. The Church's long defection ends. A new consciousness of sin is awakened in the Church as well as in the individual. There passes over the Church a wave of deep conviction and shame. Then follows a time of reformation, of purging the impurities. It seeks by united prayer and intense zeal to bring to Jesus those who do not know Him. This reformation of the Church is not sudden. The Church absorbs those large masses affected by the revival and fresh life is poured back into the hearts of its members. Actually, the fresh winds of revival may break outside the boundary or walls of the organized church, and become the spiritual fire to ignite the church, and the divine detergent to cleanse and refresh its ministry.

The second characteristic produced by a

revival movement is its joy. When the night is passed, and with it the agony of conviction and the grief and terror of sin, there breaks upon the humbled heart the peace of forgiveness. No joy on earth compares with this that awakens in the forgiven heart. People have exhausted language in trying to describe it.

At such times, Isaiah's description of the mountains and hills breaking forth into singing and all the trees of the field clapping their hands does not appear excessive. To those caught in the revival's flood, all the world seems changed. Their hearts are light, and their faces glow.

This joy is not limited to those newly converted. It fills the hearts of those who are already followers of Christ. It sweeps into the Church, making all its worship pulse and glow with spiritual fervor. This is the effect of revival, wherever it appears. It leaves in its wake numberless men and women whose faces glow with a new light and whose hearts throb with an intense and pure joy.

This new gladness characteristically finds an outlet in song. Song is the natural expression of the jubilant heart. It is the escape valve for feelings which are too exhilarating to remain silent. Most of the great leaders of revival have been poets, and the revival is born along the wings of praise. Singing has been a prominent feature in most revivals.

The conditions for revival are timeless. There are no 20th century shortcuts. In 1904, all Wales was aflame with revival. The nation had drifted far from God, and spiritual conditions were at the lowest. Church attendance was pitiably poor and practices of immorality and sinful indulgence abounded on every hand. Suddenly, through the power of prayer, like an unexpected tornado, the power of God moved in and swept over the land. Churches were crowded with three services every day lasting from 10 a.m. to 12 midnight. Evan Roberts was the human instrument God used to turn the tide of revival.

There was little preaching—mostly singing, testimonies, and prayer. There were no hymnbooks, no offerings, no advertising—but everybody sang. History records there were more songs composed than sermons delivered. Nothing had ever come over Wales with such mighty, far-reaching results.

Infidels were converted. Drunks, thieves, and thugs by the hundreds were born again. Multitudes of the most respected and socially prominent were converted. Old debts were paid, theaters and pubs closed, and the mules in the mines refused to work, being unused to the transformed attitudes of the workers, nor were they thereafter required to work on the Lord's Day.

Whatever the expression, the gladness itself is never absent. In many, it becomes so extreme that it can be dangerous. Almost every revival is accompanied by outbursts of excitement and by startling physical phenomena.

Outbreaks of physical anguish are followed by outbursts of uncontrollable joy. The effect of these extreme emotions on unstable people is often disastrous. A revival's value is not to be based on these exceptions. Many who are looking for reasons to point a finger at the movement use these cases to justify their criticisms. Those whose minds are fixed on the trivial and hearts are void of spiritual life miss the true impact of the revival on the individual soul.

All revivals affect large masses of the community. They leave a permanent influence for good behind them and create a new era in progress. All revivals start from the bottom. Their leaders are almost entirely of the people. Their greatest influence is on the poor and upon those neglected by the Church. When faith is waning, the Church loses its spirit of sacrifice. It becomes self-seeking. It uses its influence over its members to obtain comfort and ease. As a consequence, those masses of the community who are unattractive because of their ignorance and poverty are neglected.

When the news of redeeming love is proclaimed with passionate joy and conviction, the poor are reached. It is the common people who hear it with gladness. They live in poverty, neglected and uncared for by those who ought to give their lives for them. Having found little to satisfy their hunger for love, their hearts are drawn to the message of God's love. Drawn into Christianity, their hearts are uplifted by pure emotion. Their whole lives are changed, and they become an asset to the wealth of a nation. Thus, a revival means the re-creation of large portions of the community, a segment that once seemed to be a deficit to society. In the light of this fact, it would be trite to say that the next revival will be an ethical one. All revivals are ethical. They move, if authentic and sent from above, not merely in the realm of emotion but in the sphere of the conscience and the will. They leave behind them not merely joyful, but changed lives. The chains of addiction are broken. Revivals implant a new set of emotions within the heart. They inspire men and women to develop their characters and enrich their lives through education, self-discipline, and especially prayer.

The effect of a revival upon the Church is no less profound and far-reaching. For while the word *revive* literally means "to bring to life again," the word in its religious context includes the awakening of those who were dead and rejuvenating those who were alive but slumbering.

Every revival exposes the spiritual decay of the Church, with its worldliness and hypocrisy. This spiritual decay seems to move along two distinct lines.

The first tendency is for the doctrine of the Church to lose its power to convict the conscience, convince the mind, or move the heart. After a time of immense theological interest, that interest begins to wane. People's minds are attracted by fresh discoveries in other fields. Thus, theology fails to keep pace with the fresh thought of the age. It is outdated and treated with contempt by other areas of human thought, which are on the cutting edge of progress.

In addition, each age requires a restatement of truth. The truth does not change, but our comprehension of it does. We are taught to see it from new angles and with an altered perspective. Thus, there is the necessity for a new statement, for a reinterpretation of the old words in terms of the new. For words are like coins, of full value fresh from the mint, but capable of being defaced and robbed of their full value. In spiritually dead times, preachers continue to use the old words. Once so full of power, now they have no impact. This is partly because the language has changed, but also because the words have become the mere jargon of the pulpit. Preachers mumble out their clichés that have no impact on the conscience or the heart, because they themselves have ceased to be moved by them.

The Church passes through a period of skepticism. Unbelief chills its vital fires, and hypocrisy leaves its message powerless.

With the first pronouncement of the leader's living message, all this passes away. A new aspect of truth is declared, or an old and forgotten truth is restated, and suddenly people's hunger is appeased. They are fed again with the bread of life.

The second tendency in spiritual decay is for worship to become formal. The pulpit exalts ritual until the spirit is crushed. Religion is represented, not as a response of the soul to God, but as a rigid performance of outward observances and ceremonies.

Ritual forms of worship, even when elaborate, are not evil in themselves. Some people find their spiritual life enriched by them. They are not dangerous to the general worshiper as long as the spiritual life of the church is intense, and the form is the expression of the spirit. It is when the spiritual fire departs that the danger appears. The form then becomes an end in itself. Strict obedience to it becomes religion and is coldly offered to God in lieu of spiritual worship. At such times, outward observance increases rather than diminishes. The self-righteous are given opportunity to display their zeal, while they impose heavy burdens upon the hearts of the humble and the ignorant. This shift of focus, from inner life to outward observance, divorces religion from morality.

At such a time, the pastorate degenerates. The love of wealth, ease, and power appears. Ministers become the object of scorn to the skeptical and indifferent.

An example of this is the condition of Israel at the time of Christ. When the Israelites returned from the captivity, the rulers of the people turned to the Law with passionate devotion. While this devotion remained, the spiritual life of Israel was maintained. No sooner did it diminish than the minute observances of the Law became intolerable bondage. Their religion, emptied of its spiritual content, became a worship of externals. So bankrupt of spiritual discernment did the people become that the hypocrite became the popular ideal of the religious person. They had become so dead that they not only failed to recognize the Messiah, but crucified Him as a heretic.

Christ had lamented over such people—"O Jerusalem, Jerusalem, the one who kills the prophets and stones those who are sent to her! How often I wanted to gather your children together, as a hen gathers her chicks under her wings, but you were not willing!" (Matthew 23:37, NKJV).

This despiritualizing of religion, this worship of the form rather than of the spirit, is a constant threat to the Church. However, the moment the first breath of revival touches the heart of the Church, the chains which bind it are broken. With a new joy, it returns to simplicity of worship and intense sincerity of life.

8

Revivals,
the Law of Variety

The appearance of revivals owes nothing to
chance; they are a witness to God's sovereignty. Used of God for the progress of the
world, they revitalize men's and women's lives.
They appear at intervals, and at points of crisis
in individuals' lives. Although these cannot be
delineated with precision, we are able to see
a regularity in their appearance and, within
certain limits, to anticipate their coming. Next
we see that there is sufficient data to conclude
that the laws which govern them are constant
like any other of God's laws. First of all, we
perceive that they come when preparations
have been made, when the times are ripe. Next,
their appearance is signaled by certain infallible
signs, one of which is a growing discontent-
ment in individuals' hearts with corruption
and backsliding. With this, comes an intense
craving for something better. A growing spirit
of expectation that change is coming soon
develops. At last, when contributing streams
converge at a definite point, there suddenly
appears the messenger who speaks for God,

and whose voice people instantly recognize and obey.

Another similarity is what occurs when the revival movement is set in motion. When the voice of the leader is heard, vast forces, which seem to have been lying dormant, are awakened. The revival spreads like fire, and huge numbers of people are affected. Wherever it goes, and into whatever heart it enters, it creates an overwhelming realization of sin— then confession. With the forgiveness of sin comes a joy that expresses itself in song. The main effect of the revival is felt in the inner life. It awakens new spiritual emotions. It sharpens lives into subjection to the will of God. It brings the Church back to simplicity, sincerity, and a renewed spiritual vitality.

As in all of God's dealings with His creation, there are the elements of the mysterious. No two revivals are identical. While possessing common elements, every expression of each law contains unique characteristics. Each is adapted to the need of the times. It is modified first by the conditions of the age, secondly by nationality, and then by the individual characteristics of its leader. This outward variety is a necessity for success. Were all revivals identical, the majority of the people would remain unaffected. Variety is a source of life.

A revival which affects one nation or people may have little influence upon another. In many cases where the attempt was made to duplicate a revival's characteristics, the attempt not only failed, but also stirred up irritation and strife.

An illustration of this fact may be discovered in the history of the Reformation in the sixteenth century. That movement, which profoundly affected the Teutonic races, left the Latin races almost unaffected. Its geographical area was so pronounced that it still remains, and the chasm which it created still separates the Roman Catholics from the Protestants.

Another fact about revival movements is the variety in the character of their appeal. Sometimes that appeal moves in the realm of the affection. Emotional revivals are, of all revivals, the most immediately effective and the least enduring. Sometimes a revival's chief characteristic is theological, emerging in the discovery of some new truth. Each adapts itself to the urgent need of the age, and thus produces the most permanent results. Each wins its way because of its adaptation to the needs of the times and to the temperament of the people. What is effective for one cannot be effective for all.

One other significant fact regarding the variety in revivals is that movement in one direction is often followed by a movement in an opposite one. In religion, as in politics, there are two distinct camps, liberal and conservative. The watchword of the one is Freedom, that of the other is Authority. The conflict between the two is constant, but each represents too deep a factor of human life to destroy the other. Thus, a revival which carries to one extreme will be followed by a countermovement in the other direction.

Striking as the similar points are in revivals, there are also as many illustrations of variety. The same laws are in each, but as with all the laws of God, there is adaptation and readjustment.

9

Revivals,
the Law of Recoil

Every revival has a time limit. It has its day,
then it recedes. Luther set the limit to a revival
at thirty years, Isaac Taylor at fifty. Rarely does
it last beyond a generation. But in duration two
revivals are rarely alike. Because of the vari-
ables and their different characters, the extent
and duration are varied. The constant factor is
that, whatever the size of the wave, it has its
limits marked out for it.

Many people are swept into a revival's current by yielding to emotion, while their natures
remain unchanged. They cool down and are
swept back into the world again. Nothing can
be said about the percentage who fall away.
Revival movements differ in this also. In
revivals where emotions are held in check and
the appeal is made to the conscience, the effect
is more permanent.

The good effect of a revival runs on long
after the surprise and emotion are gone. Yet
there comes a time when this seems to end,
and the movement falls into decay. It becomes
not an influence for good, but for evil. Instead of

liberating, it becomes an agent of oppression. Few things in life are more pathetic than how quickly the good gets tarnished or corrupted. Such was the case with the recoil that came after the days of Luther, with its bitterness and rivalries.

In all revival movements, this law of recoil must be recognized in order to be wisely and prayerfully anticipated. A wider knowledge of such movements will prepare the Church for this, and thus its dangers can be minimized. It is the ebb of the wave which falls back, only to gain strength to push further on. When each revival has made its original contribution to the wealth of human experience, it falls back to give place to something else. There is no need to mourn. As Tennyson truthfully said, "The old order changeth, yielding place to new, and God fulfills Himself in many ways, lest one good custom should corrupt the world."

This longing for a fresh movement from God was expressed most succinctly by the Psalmist: "Oh, revive us! Then your people can rejoice in you again" (Psalm 85:6, TLB). We echo that longing when we read of past revivals, then fall to our knees and cry, "Do it again, Lord. Do it again!"

10

Revivals, the Law of the Theology of Revivals

It is important for us to know what the great doctrines have been which have awakened people to new life in past centuries.

First of all, we see that all revivals fall back upon simplicity. They cut through the accumulated doctrines and subtle complexities, until they arrive at some aspect of truth which has become forgotten or has been buried by tradition.

In perspective, every revival goes back to apostolic times and to the spirit of the early Church. Each attempts to strip the Church and the individual of the heavy burdens imposed in a time of decay, a time when men and women are more intent on *proving* the doctrines of the Church than on living them. Its central effort is to get back to the source of life.

When we analyze the messages in those great days of revival, we see one message which is never absent, a message which is at the heart of every movement. This is the message of the Cross.

How much we need the focus of the apostle

Paul: "But God forbid that I should glory except in the cross of our Lord Jesus Christ, by whom the world has been crucified to me, and I to the world" (Galatians 6:14, NKJV).

In every case where the life of the Church has become powerless, it will be found that the message of the Cross has either been denied or forgotten.

If this is true, and it is, then its value is of the utmost importance. It shows that, whenever men's and women's hearts are profoundly moved, they turn to the Cross for satisfaction, with the same instinct with which a child in need turns to its mother. Redeeming love is the message underlying every great spiritual movement of the Church. Never has there been a spiritual movement in the Christian Church in which Christ has not been realized as the source of life. Every revival is a return to Christ. Each comes from a fresh recognition of His power to save.

In the time of the Reformation, the doctrine of justification by faith had ceased to exist. Ecclesiasticism so dominated people's minds that they were blind to the truth when reading Paul's epistles. This is a curious fact about the human mind, that it has the power only to see what agrees with current opinion. Every age is imprisoned in its own conceptions and has to be set free by the minds which refuse to be enslaved.

There is a vast difference in the ways people hold the same doctrines. They are held either as supreme, or as of secondary importance. It makes all the difference in the life of the Church when prominence is given to the essential doctrines. The Church is revived when it is brought back to Christ, when it takes up the Cross again. With the message of salvation burning in its heart, it goes out once again as its Master did "to seek and to save them that are lost."

Also, it is a significant fact that no religious system which rejects the Cross knows anything of revivals in the same way that Christianity does. Their ranks are recruited from those who become skeptical in the days of depression. They are never flooded with enthusiastic life, nor charged with messages which move large amounts of people to the knowledge of divine things.

11

Revivals, the Law of the Coming Movement

Let us close with a glance into the future. With the help of these stated biblical principles, we will ask what the future has in store. Before we can do this, we must first examine the present condition of the Church and read the signs of our times.

First of all, no one pretends that all is well with the Church today. When allowance is made for exaggeration, there are enough problems left to arouse deep soul searching. On every side, there is complaint of the Church's loss of spiritual power, the increasing indifference of its people, and a decrease in membership. Where there is not decline, there is a conscious arrest of her influence, and in the world a hostility to her claims.

The Church is still active. Never was there more activity and less result. There is abundant energy, but it is not conquering energy conscious of its power, but feverish energy, conscious of its impotence. The message of the pulpit has largely lost its power to convince, and the preacher his power to lead to conversion.

When we look beneath the surface, we see much to account for this. We have been passing through an age of commercialism. Never in the history of the world have the hearts of individuals been set with such a passion upon materialism. This has deadened men's and women's hearts to the Gospel. But this is not the sole reason. The Church itself has not escaped from materialism's corruption. It has been allowed to creep in and devitalize the Church's spiritual witness.

A new conscience is arising which is judging the Church by new standards. People are growing conscious of a contradiction between Christ's attitude toward the poor and the attitude of those who profess to be Christians. There is a growing sense of social injustice. Indignation is rising because, in the presence of this, the Church has remained silent—ignoring those who need it the most.

Much of this accusation is undeserved and can be repudiated by individual congregations. But concerning the Church in general, it is impossible to deny it. Because of this, many are making sacrificial efforts to rectify their attitudes, though they know that the Church is not behind them.

Another reason for the present state of impotence arises because we have gone through an age of theological unrest. Our foundations are shifting. It is an age of transition, and such periods are ones of suffering. This unrest in the area of belief has arisen through the scientific revival which has characterized this century. The progress has been amazing. But no area of human thought has been more threatened than theology. The theory of evolution has challenged the whole Christian creed and has demanded a reevaluation of its essential beliefs. Historic research dealing with the Bible has left nothing unexamined which was once considered too holy to touch.

For many, the result of these changes has been the unsettlement of belief; for others, the loss of their faith. For all, an uncertainty regarding even the most central doctrines has arisen. These changes have introduced into the pulpit an insecurity brought about by preachers who were not quite certain of their ground. A tendency to leave many of the disputed doctrines alone and rely upon moral precepts and good living has arisen.

The result is that much, if not all, of the message of Christianity has been silenced. Passion is simulated. Energy is directed toward useless things. People in the pew are unconsciously affected by the absence of certainty, and of intense conviction. So pulpit and pew are united in a common misgiving. People find it easy to drift from the Church. Their consciences are unaffected by their relapse, because there is not the atmosphere of reality which makes neglecting the Church a sin.

If this is true, then it is a fact which should awaken the dullest heart concerned about the welfare of the world and his or her own spiritual life. Of course, a weakening Church means that the forces working against the Church are growing stronger. It makes us turn to the future and ask, "What is before us? Is the day of the Church over? Must we live on to see the decline, until it results in death?"

From such questions we can turn away with a smile. The Church is not on the eve of destruction. It is on the eve of a revival. Like the day that comes when the long night is over, so every revival comes after times of tribulation. Nothing in the world is more certain than this. The question is not "if," but "when." Regarding such a question, it would be impious to speak with authority. It is not for us to know the times which God has hidden. At the same time, there is much to give us hope.

When we turn to the present social and political conditions, it is not difficult to see that a great revolution is taking place. There is emerging a multitude of the neglected, demanding recognition, justice, and human rights. A new cry is heard today. The cry not only pierces the halls of government, but echoes like a wail in our churches. It is the cry of those who are awakening to a sense of bitter wrong and of social discontent. As crude as their cry may be, it is valid. People are coming to the recognition that the poor and deprived are men and women made in the image of God, thus having value.

All awakenings are dangerous if unattended by spiritual illumination and allowed to grow in hostility to religion. As a rule, today's leaders are often not found in the Church. They are standing outside the Church, accusing it of betraying God. Whether this is true or not is irrelevant, only this pathetic and humiliating fact of history has to be recalled: nearly every great revival has originated outside of the Church. This may not happen today, but in times of degeneracy, the Spirit of Christ is often found outside of the Church. Again, when the Spirit is freshly poured out, it is not the Church, but those outside it who make the first response. Only afterward is the Church awakened.

The Church today appears helpless to cope with its growing responsibilities. The problems are so great that the Church seems to sink under the weight of them. It is the Church's duty, not to solve the problems, but to give an inspiration. It is a flood of new spiritual life that is needed. When the heart is alive, the hardest problem becomes solvable. Love awakes and finds its own channels. It is the Church's coldness that makes problems unsolvable.

The solution is a revival of spiritual religion—a new breath which will pass over the valley of dry bones and make them live. The world is ready for this revival, whether or not the Church is. For the Church, revival means humiliation, a bitter knowledge of unworthiness, and an open and humiliating confession of sin. It comes to scorch before it heals.

This is why revival has been unpopular with many within the Church. It says nothing to them of the power they have learned to love, the ease, or success. It accuses them of sin; it tells them that they are dead. It calls them to forsake all else and follow Christ.

Is the Church today ready to hear that voice? Some doubt it. It is upon the hearts of the few that the agony falls. Revivals are not preceded by the Church becoming aware of the need, but by a few people here and there, who, feeling the need, begin to entreat God for a revival. This sense of need grows into a burden, until the cry becomes an agony. This is the cry which God cannot deny.

No revival can come from below. All attempts to create a revival fail. Nor can we bring a revival down, since prayer is not the cause of a revival, but the human preparation for one. By prayer we prepare the soil.

Is there a disposition to pray for revival? Are devout men and women everywhere becoming alarmed, not for the success of the Church, but for the glory of Christ? If not, then the night is not far spent, a deeper darkness is yet to come. For what use would a revival be, if we were not prepared for it? It would pass over us without doing its work. J. Hudson Taylor affirmed this when he wrote, "The spirit of prayer is, in essence, the spirit of revival."

But there are signs that this burden to pray is being laid upon the souls of men and women. Many are beginning to passionately long for better things and to agonize in prayer. To fail in this is to be a traitor to Christ and to the deepest need of the world around us.

Encouragement that the dawn is near comes from another side. Some have pointed out that we have been passing through an age of criticism, when much of the accepted truth has not been able to stand the test. Most careful onlookers are convinced that the worst is over. The destructive era has ended and the constructive era has begun. A great change has overcome the leaders of science and of thought. There is a new reverence for the spiritual life, and thought has drifted far from the agnostic position.

One of the most significant facts connected with this new movement is the orthodox position. Much has changed, but nothing vital in Christian belief has been lost. The old lives still in the new. With the recognition of the spiritual reality, it is possible to return to that same sense of security of belief which makes a revival of religion possible. As long as belief was uncertain and those responsible to defend the Church's faith were panic-stricken, this was impossible. With the new confidence, there is also arising a longing for a revived Church.

It is encouraging that this dryness is only local. In other parts of the world, the wave that is subsiding here is flowing in full force. In Asia, Latin America, and Africa, Christianity is spreading rapidly. But not only there is

Christianity growing, but also in Eastern
Europe the growth is remarkable.

Of what character will the next revival be?
No one can say, but there are certain things
that we can hope for; others we may regard
with certainty. First of all, no revival would be
worth anything if it excluded those who are
alienated from the Church. Whatever the message is, it must bring the people back to their
heritage within the Church. It must bring the
Church back to the needs of the poor and
underprivileged. Such a message will demand
a greater sacrifice than the Church has been
called to make since its birth. For it was not
power and position which won the hearts of
the poor and outcast in those days, but it was
the Church's poverty and love.

The next revival will move us toward unity,
which goes along with the spirit of our age.
Denominationalism is breaking down around
us. In the face of the complexities of modern
life, the cry for unity is heard. All that is
needed is the increase of love that comes with
revival, to cement those unions already
formed.

Whatever form the coming awakening may
take, we may be certain that it will bring us
back to the essentials. This is the result of
every true revival. It cuts through the trap-
pings until it gets to the core of life. It leads
men and women back to simplicity. When the
heart earnestly seeks God, it takes the shortest
route. Above all, it will bring us back to Christ.

The day may be near. Even now He may be preparing His messenger.

" *'But who can endure the day of His coming? And who can stand when He appears? For He is like a refiner's fire and like fuller's soap. He will sit as a refiner and a purifier of silver; He will purify the sons of Levi, and purge them as gold and silver, that they may offer to the Lord an offering in righteousness. Then the offering of Judah and Jerusalem will be pleasant to the Lord, as in the days of old, as in former years. And I will come near you for judgment; I will be a swift witness against sorcerers, against adulterers, against perjurers, against those who exploit wage earners and widows and the fatherless, and against those who turn away an alien—because they do not fear Me,' says the Lord of hosts."*

"But to you who fear My name the Sun of Righteousness shall arise with healing in His wings; and you shall go out and grow fat like stall-fed calves."

—Malachi 3:2–5; 4:2, NKJV

Notes

Notes

Notes

Notes

Notes

Notes

Notes